Nonfiction

"Row, row, row your boat, gently down the stream, merrily, merrily, merrily, merrily, life is but a dream." Perhaps you recall singing this song numerous times while traveling with a group of friends, or while gathered around a campfire. Perhaps like me, you have wondered about the theme of this simple rhyme, and pondered its philosophical message. Can it be applied to life? Most people will contend going with the flow, gently down the stream, of life is desirable and rewarding when possible. However we must realize that life dictates, like salmon fulfilling their destiny by swimming upstream against the currents of water to eventually spawn. We must struggle against the adversaries of life to find fulfillment and eventually discover our destiny.

To find fulfillment and discover our destiny, we need to ask the question, "Why?" Why are circumstances as they are? Why is nature as it is? And why, why, why are we humans here on earth?

In his book titled "A Brief History of Time", professor Hawking's last statement reads, **"however, if we do discover a complete theory, it should in time be understandable in broad principle by everyone, not just a few scientists. Then we shall all, philosophers, scientists, and just ordinary people, be able to take part in the discussion of the question of why it is that we and the universe exist. If we find the answer to that, it would be the ultimate triumph of human reason. For then we would know the mind of God."** *I would like to take this opportunity to thank Professor Hawking for giving his permission to quote this statement.*

It is the endeavor of this book to present a philosophy of life and explain it in logical terms that will be understandable in broad principle by everyone. Why, the universe and we exist and explore and discover our nature and circumstances.

Does God exist? What's the purpose of life? Basically, what's going on? When we ask these questions we are implying the existence of God. Otherwise these inquiring questions would not enter our consciousness. There would be no reason to ponder the subject. Our basic needs to exist are food and shelter, which we can acquire without the knowledge of God. What we are implying is that there must be more to life than these basic needs. Actually, life as we know it is very fragile and completely dependent on stringent external control of the natural environment. For example, the temperature range, which life requires to exist in, is minute when compared to possible extremes of temperature. Even within this minute temperature range most of life depends upon a critical fluctuating temperature. The wind is another example of stringent control. What keeps the wind from blowing constantly? What keeps the wind currents from gusting to hundreds or even thousands of miles per hour? Would life, as we know it be able to continue under these circumstances? And doesn't it seem strange and miraculous in this vast open atmosphere of space, we live in, that the wind currents could be calm for even a few moments. Yet a calm environment does exist and is the general rule rather than the exception.

In its orbit around the sun, the earth tilts at just the right angle and as a result the season on earth changes. Later it tilts back and the season changes again. We plan for these changes, and our existence depends upon the seasonal fall harvest of crops as well as the seasonal spring thaw. Does the earth orbit the sun in an uncontrolled sporadic manner? Is the orbital tilt of the earth just a cosmic twitch? Some people would rather take a narrow demented view that a big bang occurred and fate put the universe in just the right setting, then time, with its so-called intelligence, made everything else evolve.

Wake up! If our environment wasn't controlled it would be in total chaos. Isn't it obvious and don't we prove by the societies we humans establish that they are only as stable as the control we instill, enforce, and abide by? Even the steady rhythm of the heart beating and our rhythmic breathing speak of control. If either of these natural functions deviates from their symmetry, we instinctively realize that stringent order and control are necessary if we are to continue to exist. Life sustains life. All life is dependent upon life to exist. The ecological balance and the propagation of life prove this statement to be true. The honeybee, for example, depends upon the flower for honey and the flower depends upon the bee for pollination. This also illustrates how life had to be created simultaneously in order for the dependency of life on life to be possible. It is also difficult to conclude that the metamorphosis of caterpillars and some insects could simply evolve or instinct with its inborn tendency to perform certain acts of survival could come into existence with no plan or intelligence. How can we accept a theory that the chameleon, cuddle fish, and octopus can change color by accident or with nothing except the environment to create this spontaneous phenomenon. Are we so naïve? If all these functions are possible without intelligence, why hasn't man with his intellectual ability been able to duplicate and improve on these natural inborn abilities?

In this era of time, man is identifying, documenting and counting the many thousands and thousands of different species of plants insects, birds, and animals, and guess what, almost daily a new life form is discovered. Is it plausible, like the universe with its countless number of stars, that the variety of life on earth is infinite? What about the big bang theory? How can it fit in with the creationists' explanation? The Big Bang speaks of infinite power, infinite vision, and infinite knowledge. What a profound and marvelous opening statement. Or, perhaps, we could say, each panoramic moment of each day is a unique, once-in-an-infinite-time miracle.

The Holy Bible has been compiled into a book from writings over thousands of years and yet it's the same author. Who else except an eternal God could have been the author? It seems silly and trivial to question such obvious conclusions concerning God's creation. In The Living Bible we read, **"The Heavens are telling the glory of God. They are a marvelous display of his craftsmanship. Day and night they keep telling about God. Without a sound or word silent in the sky. Their message reaches out to all the world."**

This is a quote from The Living Bible, Psalms Chapter 19:1-4, and is used by permission of the Teledyne Publishing House, Inc., Wheaten IL, 60189. Copyright 1971. All rights reserved. Quotes will be noted by the title of The Living Bible or may be noted by the initials (TLB).

In spite of these obvious conclusions, an element of doubt concerning God's creation does exist. Predictable and logical conclusions seem to indicate a sequential evolution of life and a possible chance existence. Certain natural phenomenon leads us to reason and develop theories concerning life and the formation of our universe. The vast majority of people do not question the theory that life has evolved and adapted to the environment in order to survive. However, the opposite reasoning is the only sure way for life to continue. The natural environment must be controlled, by an inelegance of the universe, in order for life to survive.

While contemplating the evolution theory, I came to the conclusion that the 80/20 Rule applies. Eighty percent of evolution theory is apparition and twenty percent is imagination. Have you noticed how often the evolution theory implies the word **appear** to explain the origin of the universe and the evolution of life? First, the universe appeared, and within the universe the planets including our earth appeared. Then light appeared. Then order appeared. Then the laws of nature appeared. Then life appeared, and it appeared to evolve and eventually man appeared with all of his built-in complexities of appearances, such as eye sight, hearing, smelling, tasting, feeling, all the emotions, intellect, equilibrium, dexterity, not to mention the appearance of his soul consisting of the appearance of reasoning, imagination, affections, memory and conscience.

As we, observe and experience life perpetually deteriorating into oblivion, it should naturally arouse a desire to search for alternative explanations. In the final analysis, if we conclude that evolution theories are unreasonable, incomplete and questionable, it certainly behooves us to step forward and search for alternative explanations of life.

The natural human process of reasoning, logic, and imagination, produces doubt concerning the creation. Doubt is what keeps us from becoming aware of reality. Attitude is everything. The willingness to consider other possibilities is the key to understanding, discernment and insight. To prove the existence of God we must move forward beyond our natural senses of reasoning and imagination and we use faith to achieve understanding. ***"By faith, by believing God, we know that the world and the stars, in fact all things were made at God's command and that they were all made from things that can't be seen."*** **Hebrews 11:3 (TLB)** As mentioned before, human reasoning and imagination produces doubt concerning God and his creation. Well, doubt is replaced by confidence and assurance when we begin to use faith. Perhaps you have heard the expression, "seeing is believing, or show me and I'll believe it." Well, when contemplating God's spiritual world, we turn this saying around **"Believing is seeing."** Seeing, in this sense, is to comprehend, understand, and grasp the meaning intended. By exercising and using the 'believing is seeing' rule, it produces spiritual insight. Faith is the all-important factor that allows us to become aware of and personally acquainted with God. By believing we please God, and this is the link that joins us together with him. This faith element is part of what God is referring to when he created man like himself. In Genesis, 1:26 (TLB), it says, ***"Then God said, 'Let us make a man, someone like ourselves to be the master of all life upon the earth and in the sky and in the sea'."***

Those who live by faith are masters of all life because man is the only living creature on earth that has the ability to establish a personal relationship with God and please him by exercising and using faith. In The Living Bible we read ***"You can never please God without faith, without depending on him, anyone who wants to come to God, must believe that there is a God and that he rewards those who sincerely look for him."*** **Hebrews 11:6.** When we begin to exercise the seed of faith, we experience an awakening or an awareness of God's spiritual world. 2Corinthians 5:7 (TLB); ***"We know that these things are true <u>by believing, not by seeing</u>."*** The kingdom of God is not visible to the natural man. It is brought into awareness by the revelation and inspiration of God as a result of exercising faith. The spiritual world exists and grows by using the formula **"believing is seeing."** What is faith? In the King James Bible (KJV) Hebrews Chapter 11 reads; ***"Now faith is the substance of things hoped for, the evidence of things not seen."*** Faith brings the spiritual world into reality it is the confidence and assurance that something we want is going to happen. When a person comes to the conclusion that there is strong evidence and an overwhelming possibility that God does exist, this person is in an ideal position to exercise this seed of faith. If this person takes the first step of faith by accepting as fact the existence of God, he or she will experience an awakening, within the heart, of God's existence, thus the evidence is experienced and becomes a reality to the individual. When a person accepts by faith the existence of God, this person will certainly agree, that **"believing is truly seeing."**

Although the Bible is regarded as the infallible word of God, it appears to be a book of myth, fables and contradictions. The reason, it appears to be contradictory, and confusing, is because it is a spiritual book written by people who are under the inspiring influence of God's spirit. Read 2Timothy 3:16 (In the King James Bible) (KJ). ***"All scripture is given by inspiration of God."***

We humans try to use our natural senses of reasoning and logic to interpret the meaning of the Bible. God explains why we must interpret his words spiritually in 1 Corinthians 2:11-13 (TLB) we read; ***"No one can really know what anyone else is thinking or what he is really like except that person himself. And no one can know God's thoughts except God's own spirit. And God has actually given us his spirit, (not the world's spirit) to tell us about the wonderful free gifts of grace and blessing that God has given us. In telling you about these gifts, we have even used the very words given to us by the Holy Spirit, not words that we as men might choose. So we use the Holy Spirit's words to explain the Holy Spirit's facts."*** In the King James Bible, Proverbs 3:5; ***"Trust in the Lord with all thine heart and lean not unto thine own understanding."*** And in The Living Bible, Isaiah 55:8-9; ***"This plan of mine is not what you would work out, neither are my thoughts the same as yours. For as the heavens are higher than the earth, so are my ways higher than yours and my thoughts than yours."***

God exists in the supernatural realm. His works and the results are always **miraculous, mysterious and unbelievable.** For example, in this perpetually changing world we live in, the only thing perfect is imperfection. And yet many individual segments are unbelievably unique and miraculously similar. Of all the countless stars in the universe, no two are exactly alike. Each pebble of sand, on the beach, has a singular unique geometric design infinitely different from every other pebble. And yet it unmistakably resembles collectively all the other pebbles of sand found on the beach. These examples may seem so obvious and simple, that they appear to be laced with wild imaginings and are like trivia with no appreciable intellectual value or, in one word, *unbelievable.* In The Living Bible we read, Ecclesiastics 11:15 ***"God's ways are as mysterious as pathways of the wind and as a manner in which a human spirit is infused into a little body of a baby while it is yet in its mother".***

Isn't it amazing that the most brilliant scientific minds of evolution can spend a lifetime studying the past to try and explain the mysteries of nature and the universe, while an ordinary person with a childlike attitude can comprehend the simple logic, of creation? Look in The Living Bible, St. Luke 10:21. ***"Then He, (Jesus) was filled with the joy of the Holy Spirit and said I praise you oh Father of Heaven and earth for hiding these things from the intellectuals and the worldly wise and for revealing them to those who are as trusting as little children. Yes,*** *thank you Father for that is the way you wanted it."* Also, in Luke 18:17 (TLB); *"For the kingdom of God belongs to men who have hearts as trusting as these little children. And any one who doesn't have their kind of faith will never get within the kingdoms gates."*

Hopefully, part of the original questions are answered, 'Why the universe exists?' Isn't it to show God's majesty and infinite control and don't we all on a clear night gaze in amazement and marvel at the host of heavenly splendor. *"He merely spoke and the heavens were formed and all the galaxies of stars"* Psalms 33:6 (TLB).

Chapter 2.

When a person has experienced a spiritual awakening, there is an inner urge and desire to inquire and learn more about God and His eternal plan. This inquiring urge is a personal assurance that the individual has become aware of and by faith is beginning to see God's spiritual world. As we discuss, ponder, reason, and accept God's word, we become more and more aware of God's spiritual Kingdom of Heaven. Most people who believe in heaven think of it as the hereafter, but those who are spiritually aware realize that this is a present tense experience. We can experience and enter, spiritually, God's Kingdom while still alive in the natural body.

This spiritual world, the kingdom of Heaven, is not necessarily a mystical world that requires us to go into a trance-like state of mind, special mood, or any other extraordinary condition. All we need is an inquiring attitude and a willingness to consider explanations other than what we may now think, profess or believe. This inquisitive attitude is interpreted and described as a "humble spirit". Read Matthew Chapter 5, Verse3 in the Living Bible. *"Humble men are very fortunate, He told them, for the kingdom of Heaven is given to them*. Also Psalms Chapter 69, Verse32 in the Living Bible says, *"The humble shall see their God at work for them."*

The works of God are so simple and obvious that any human being is able to comprehend, and yet it's incomprehensible to self-taught minds. The complexities and depth of understanding of God is most perplexing and difficult to sort out and conclude logically. Only with the inspiring spirit of God can we hope to puzzle together the mysteries of God's spiritual world.

To understand our human nature and our circumstances, it is necessary to start at the beginning. The Holy Bible Chapter One tells about the creation of heaven, earth, and man. In the King James Version Chapter One, Verse 26, God says: ***"Let us make a man in our image after our likeness"*** etc. Then in the 27th Verse, ***"So God created man in His own image, in the image of God created He him; male and female created He them."*** Then finally in Genesis 2:1-3, ***"Thus the heavens and earth were finished and all the host of them. And on the seventh day God ended His work that he had made. And He rested on the Seventh day from all his work that He had made. And God blessed the seventh day and sanctified it: because that in it He had rested from all His work which God created and made."*** In these three verses Genesis 2: 1-3, it is reported four times that God had finished the creation, and the fourth time mentioned He emphasizes the finished creation by resting *"from all His work which God created and made."* The first chapter and the first three verses of the second chapter of Genesis is a complete explanation of God's spiritual creation and its conclusion. Notice: after the spiritual creation is completed, God does something else.

In the King James Bible Genesis Chapter 2 Verse 7, ***"and the Lord God formed man of the dust of the ground and breathed into his nostrils the breath of life and man became a living soul"***. Therefore, we see that the man and woman created in the first chapter of Genesis Verse 27 is a spiritual creation, and the man (Adam) "formed of the dust of the ground" Chapter Two, Verse 7 is a living soul, a natural physical being. As we shall see, Gods plan is for the natural man and their relationship to gravitate towards, and fulfill, the spiritual creation of Genesis Chapter One.

After forming man from the earth, God offers man (Adam and Eve) a way to maintain a pleasant relationship with Him by allowing their obedience to determine the duration of this relationship. God does this by placing a tree of life and a tree of conscience among other trees in a garden (explained in Genesis Chapter Two). Then God commanded the man (Adam) Genesis 2: 16-17 King James Bible, ***"of every tree of the garden thou mayest freely eat. But of the tree of knowledge of good and evil, thou shall not eat of it. For in the day thou eatest thereof, thou shalt surely die."***

At this period in time, man (Adam and Eve) had a perpetual carefree life because of the fruit from the tree of life. This period of time for man was "Utopia" in its purest form. Then in Genesis 3: 3 of the King James Bible, Eve is tricked into eating the forbidden fruit, but Adam knew exactly what he was about to do. Adam realized that he must choose to associate himself with God or Eve (Eve had eaten the forbidden fruit, which, at this moment in time, separated her from Adam and God). Adam had declared in Genesis 2: 23 - 24 of the King James Bible, ***"this is it. She is part of my own bone and flesh. Therefore shall a man leave his father and mother and shall cleave to his wife and they shall be one flesh"***. (God is Adam's father and mother)

Adam thought carefully about being disobedient, but decided to separate himself from God in order to be one with Eve. He chose to be with Eve regardless of the consequences. First Timothy 2:14 King James Bible says, ***"Adam was not deceived"***. As a result of our ancestor's disobedience, we have inherited a disobedient nature. We are susceptible to transgress God's will (Eve) and we willingly transgress God's will (Adam). Consequently, we can read about the results of our ancestors' nature by reading in the Living Bible Romans Chapter 5, Verse 12, ***"When Adam sinned, sin entered the entire human race. His sin spread death throughout all the world, so everything began to grow old and die, for all sinned."*** Nature transformed and began to experience a perpetual, repetitious cycle of death. The natural world adapted to man's rebellious nature. We humans cannot exist in a tranquil environment. Our wants are endless. We strive for competition. We thrive on a need for perpetual problems, and our achievements, goals and ambitions are only partially satisfied as a result of problem solving.

In contrast to God's spiritual world, our nature is explained in the book of Romans Chapter 7, Verse 14-17 (TLB). ***"The law is good then, and the trouble is not there but with me, because I am sold into slavery with sin as my owner. I don't understand myself at all, for I really want to do what is right, but I can't. I do what I don't want to – what I hate. I know perfectly well that what I am doing is wrong, and my bad conscience proves that I agree with these laws I am breaking. But I can't help myself, because I'm no longer doing it. It is sin inside me that is stronger than I am that makes me do these evil things."***

To explain this conflicting nature, for example, one of God's commandments is "Thou shall not lie." When confronted with the possibility of lying, I am instantly aware within myself of a desire to avoid the consequences of the truth by exercising the option to deceive by lying. This awareness of deception confirms that I agree with the commandment "Thou shall not lie." It should be noted here that the option to lie or not is part of our nature, whether we actually tell a lie or not. It is also necessary to realize that our thoughts we have are what God judges us by, regardless of whether we act on these thoughts or not. In Mark Chapter 7, Verse 16 (TBL)- *"Your souls aren't harmed by what you eat, but by what you think and say."* Then Verse 20 states, *"And he added 'It is the thought – life that pollutes.'"* Also Matthew 5:28 in the Living Bible states, *"But I say: Anyone who even looks at a woman with lust in his eye has already committed adultery with her in his heart."*

Continuing with Romans 7: 18 – 25 (TLB), *"I know I am rotten through and through so far as my old sinful nature is concerned. No matter which way I turn, I can't make myself do right. I want to, but I can't. When I want to do good, I don't; and when I try not to do wrong, I do it anyway. Now if I am doing what I don't want to do, it is plain where the trouble is: sin still has me in its evil grasp. It seems to be a fact of life that when I want to do what is right, I inevitably do what is wrong. I love to do God's will so far as my new nature is concerned, but there is something else deep within me, in my lower nature, that is at war with my mind and wins the fight and makes me a slave to the sin that is still within me. In my mind I want to be God's willing servant, but instead I find myself still enslaved to sin".*

Hopefully, this example of a personal experience will explain the sin nature. Many years ago while trying to be obedient to God by using human reasoning and human imagination, I thought it necessary to pray each night before retiring. I would pray asking forgiveness for being angry, upset, and generally all negative human feelings that would create an undesirable image. Using the previous example of "Thou shall not lie," I would also recall, to the best of my memory, the time during the day that I was tempted to lie, the lies, if any, I had told and any lie I might have forgotten. This act of praying soon became a methodical, repetitious pretense. Consequently, I felt miserable and frustrated all the time. Often pondering this dilemma and constantly asking why, the answer finally dawned upon me and I prayed one last time. This final prayer went something like this: "Dear God, please forgive me for I am a liar." Guess what? I finally told the truth. What a precious jewel in the puzzle of life. It fits exactly and makes this part of the Book of Romans crystal clear. Look in the Living Bible Psalms 51, Verse 5 and 6. *"But I was born a sinner, yes, from the moment my mother conceived me. You deserve honestly from the heart; yes, utter sincerity and truthfulness. Oh, give me this wisdom."* Next read Psalms 32, Verse 3, 4, and 5. *"There was a time when I wouldn't admit what a sinner I was. But my dishonesty made me miserable and filled my days with frustration. All day and all night Your hand was heavy on me. My strength evaporated like water on a sunny day until I finally admitted all my sins to You and stopped trying to hide them. I said to myself, 'I will confess them to the Lord' and You forgave me! All my guilt is gone."*

It is important to realize and accept the fact that the inherited Adam and Eve nature never changes, except perhaps to get worse. Quoting from the Living Bible Romans Chapter 8, Verse 7, *"…because the old sinful nature within us is against God. It never did obey God's laws and it never will"*. It is also important to realize that the old nature and the new spiritual nature are distinct, separate natures and cannot merge." But as we shall see, in chapter four, there are forces in our natural world that attempt to merge the two natures together. Quoting again from the Living Bible Galatians Chapter 5, Verse 17 and 18: *"…for we naturally love to do evil things that are just the opposite form the things the Holy Spirit tells us to do." And the good things we want to do when the Holy Spirit has his way with us are just the opposite of our natural desires* (our natural desires are trying to be good, i.e. [that is], attempt to keep from lying rather than admit to being a liar.) *These two forces within us are constantly fighting each other to win control over us, and our wishes are never free from their pressures. When you are guided by the Holy Spirit, you need no longer force yourself to obey Jewish laws"*. This includes all modern, moral, ethical, religious and patriotic man-made opinions, rules and laws. These man-made rules and laws may have some significant value to the individual while here on earth, but they have no eternal value. We are not accountable to God for man-made opinions, rules, and laws.

So here we are with a nature that opposes God, and we might ask, "What part does this play in the puzzle of life? How can a sinful nature have any positive value?" There is an illustration that comes to mind that will shed some light of this situation. A speaker was showing an audience a scenic picture of mountains, grass, and trees. The colors were vivid. The picture was excellent in every detail, but there was something missing. For some reason the picture looked flat and unreal. No one in the audience could tell what was wrong until the host pointed out that the shadows were missing. So we see that the shadows give life to the picture, and our life on earth gives understanding or depth to the spiritual life. For example, how could we know and appreciate life if we had not experienced death? How could we know real joy if we had not known sorrow? How could we be grateful for love if we had not been subjected to hate? How could we appreciate being found if we were not lost? We could go on and on with endless comparisons. In conclusion, a spiritual person is experiencing the shadows of life here on earth. .

Chapter 3

Who is Jesus? Jesus asked his disciples, *"Who are the people saying I am?"* **Matthew 16:13 (TLB).** *"Well, they replied, some say John the Baptist; some Elijah; some Jeremiah, or one of the other prophets. Then He asked them, who do you think I am? Simon Peter answered, The Christ, the Messiah, the Son of the living God. God has blessed you, Simon, son of Jonah, Jesus said, for my Father in heaven has personally revealed this to you--this is not from any human source".* " <u>This is not from any human source.</u>" This statement tells us that the real nature of Jesus is made known by the revelation of God's spirit.

Today, the religious world has different impressions of who Jesus is. Some regard Him as another important person in history. Some give the impression that He is a lifeless piece of meat on a cross, and others refuse to acknowledge Him in their religion. It is plain to see whom Jesus is by reading the first chapter of the gospel of John, quoting from the Living Bible, 1-5. *"Before anything else existed, there was Christ with God. He has always been alive <u>and is Himself God.</u> He created everything there is--nothing exists that He didn't make. Eternal life is in Him, and this life gives light to all mankind. His life is the light that shines through the darkness--and the darkness can never extinguish It."* Next, read verse 14 (TLB), *"And Christ became a human being and lived here on earth among us and was full of loving forgiveness and truth. And some of us have seen His glory--the glory of the only Son of the heavenly Father!"*

It is a most miraculous mind boggling, unbelievable event, to think that the One who created this vast, endless universe actually dwelt in a human body and lived among us human beings. How is this possible? ***"When I look up in the night skies and see the work of Your fingers--the moon and stars You have made, I cannot understand how You could bother with mere puny man, to pay attention to him and yet You have made him a little lower than the angels and placed a crown of glory and honor upon his head".*** *Psalms 8: 1-5 (TLB).*

Even more unbelievable is how few people realize, recognize and accept this reality. It's hard to imagine how millions and millions of intelligent people could be so completely oblivious of this most illumines event. And yet the world, as a whole, is still unimpressed by this event. And yet from time to time we are subjected to this miraculous fact and still it doesn't seem to impress us. For example, part of the lyrics of a popular song in the 90's was, **"What if God was one of us, just a slob like one of us."** Well, He was just like one of us. God even tells us that we would not recognize Jesus when He came to earth. Quoting part of Isaiah, Chapter 53 in the Living Bible, ***"<u>But, oh how few believe it!</u> Who will listen? To whom, will God reveal His saving power? In God's eyes, He was like a tender green shoot, sprouting from a root in dry and sterile ground. <u>But in our eyes there was no attractiveness at all</u>, nothing to make us want Him. <u>We despised Him and rejected Him</u>--a man of sorrows, acquainted with bitterest grief. We turned our backs on Him and looked the other way when He went by. <u>He was despised and we didn't care.</u> Yet it is our grief He bore, our sorrow that weighted Him down. <u>And we thought His troubles were punishment from God, for His own sins!</u>"***

According to the footnotes (in the Living Bible), the 53rd chapter of Isaiah was written eight hundred years before Jesus was born, which implies that no matter when He arrived in the world, He would be treated the same way. In other words, if Jesus were here on earth today, He would be treated exactly the same way as He was then. Why was Jesus so completely unrecognized? He simply didn't fit the profile of a popular person. He appeared as nothing more than a common plain human being. For example, one instance is recorded in the gospel of Luke. Jesus had made some remarks that were against the teaching of that day. In Luke 5:28-30 (TLB), **"These remarks stung them to fury and jumping up they mobbed Him and took Him to the** *edge of the hill on which the city was built, to push Him over the cliff, but He walked away through the crowd and left them".* Also, John 10:39 (TLB), *"Once again they started to arrest Him. But He walked away and left them."* He was a total stranger, unrecognizable to everyone refusing to acknowledge Him and believe His teachings. He appeared to vanish when in a group of people, just another face in the crowd, so to speak. There wasn't anything in His character to indicate He was anybody other than a carpenter's son. Only the miracle healings and His teachings revealed who He really was. Mark 6:2-3 (TBL) *"The next Sabbath he went to the synagogue to teach, and the people were astonished at his wisdom and his miracles because <u>he was just a local man like themselves</u>. 'He's no better than we are,' they said. <u>'He's just a carpenter,</u> Mary's boy, and a brother of James and Joseph, Judas and Simon. And his sisters live right here among us.' <u>And they were offended!"</u>*

This is why so few would believe who He was. For example even John the Baptist, who had pointed Jesus out to the people (John 1:31) had doubts. Matthew 11:2 (TLB) *"John the Baptist, who was now in prison, heard about all the miracles the Messiah was doing, so he sent his disciples to ask Jesus, are You really the one we are waiting for, or shall we keep on looking? Jesus told them, Go back to John and tell him about the miracles you've seen Me do. The blind people I've healed and the lame people now walking without help and the cured lepers, and the deaf who hear, and the dead raised to life; and tell him about my preaching the Good News to the poor. Then give him this message, blessed are those who don't doubt me."*

Jesus could not be recognized by sight. But he could be recognized by one of the apostles. Judas Iscariot, one of the twelve apostles, went to the chief priests and asked, *"How much will you give me to get Jesus in your hands?"* Matthew 26:14 (TLB). Then Judas says (Mark 14:44-46) *"You will know which one to arrest when I go over and greet Him. Then you can take Him easily. (45) So as soon as they arrived, he walked up to Jesus, Master he exclaimed, and embraced Him with a great show of friendliness. (46) Then the mob arrested Jesus and held Him fast."* Notice the last four words "and held him fast." They didn't want to take a chance of losing Jesus in the crowd. I mention this image of Jesus because it confirms what Isaiah records in Chapter 53; this is quoted again. *"But in our eyes there was no attractiveness at all, nothing to make us want Him. We despised Him and rejected Him--a man of sorrows* *acquainted with bitterest grief. <u>We turned our backs on Him and looked the other way when He went by. He was despised and we didn't care.</u>"*

Notice in the book of Philippians 2:6&7 (TLC) "Jesus---- ***"who Though he was God did not demand and cling to his rights as God, but laid aside his mighty power and glory, taking the <u>disguise of a slave</u> and becoming a man."*** Notice the comment "taking the disguise of a slave". A slave is a non-citizen, the lowest-class person; naturally, a slave probably couldn't hold office or be an official of any kind etc. An example of Jesus "non-citizen" states is recorded in Matthew 17: 25,26&27(TLB) ***"On their arrival in Capernaum, the Temple tax collectors came to Peter and asked him, Doesn't your master pay taxes? Of course he does," Peter replied. Then he went into the house to talk to Jesus about it, but before he had a chance to speak, Jesus asked him, "What do you think, Peter? Do kings levy assessments against their own people, or <u>against conquered foreigners?</u>" "Against the foreigners," Peter replied. "Well, then," Jesus said "the citizens are free! However, we don't want to offend them, so go down to the shore and throw in a line, and open the mouth of the first fish you catch. You will find a coin to cover the taxes for both of us, take it and pay them."***

Why would God go to all this trouble to be so completely rejected and to be punished even though He was completely and totally innocent of any wrong? Many people have memorized the answer and verse of John 3:16 (TLB) ***"For God loved the world so much that He gave His only Son so that anyone who believes in Him shall not perish but have eternal life."*** Why was it necessary to pay such a high price? Are we individually worth having our God condemned to death? We may not think so, but God has put a price on our souls. Psalms 49:8-9 (TLB) ***"<u>For a soul is far too precious to be ransomed by mere earthly wealth. There is not enough of it in all the world to buy eternal life for just one soul, to keep it out of hell.</u>"***

We might ask? How can the death of Jesus pay this tremendous price? Well, his was a perfect life; after all <u>He is God.</u> He didn't deserve to die and He didn't have to die. He willingly sacrificed Himself. Then He traded His perfect life for each individuals imperfect, corrupt life. ***"<u>For God took the sinless Christ and poured into Him our sins.</u> Then in exchange, He poured God's goodness into us."*** 2 Corinthians 5:21 (TLB).

In chapter two, it was explained how we human beings have inherited a sinful nature from our ancestors, Adam and Eve; the only way to free ourselves of this curse is to accept the exchange that God has provided, namely the sacrifice Jesus has successfully accomplished. When we accept the exchange, there is a pleasant feeling of relief and a renewed life in our heart begins. Psalms 147:11 (TLB) *"But His joy is in those who reverence [respect, believe, trust] Him, those who expect Him to be loving and kind"*.

Are you acquainted with an important person? Perhaps you are related to a historic hero or you know somebody personally who has accomplished something noteworthy. Notice how important you feel, by virtue of the acquaintance. You feel proud to be associated with the famous person. "Like a chip off of the admirable block," so to speak. When a person begins to perceive the plan of God and realize the abundant attention He gives to each individual and the extent of His love expanded for each individual, you begin to feel exalted by the association. *"God showed how much He loved us by sending his only Son into this wicked world to bring to us eternal life through His death. In this act we see what real love is, it is not our love for God but His love for us when He sent his Son to satisfy God's anger against our sins."* 1 John 4:9 (TLB)

Now, if we go to the New Testament we can read about the results of Jesus sacrifice in the Living Bible, Romans 5:15-21 *"And what a difference between man's sin and God's forgiveness! For this one man, Adam, brought death to many through his sin. But this one man, Jesus Christ, brought forgiveness to many through God's mercy. Adam's one sin brought the penalty of death to many, while Christ freely takes away many sins and gives glorious life instead. The sin of one man, Adam, caused death to be king overall, but all who will take God's gift of forgiveness and acquittal are kings of life because of this one man, Jesus Christ. Yes, Adam's sin brought punishment to all, but Christ's righteousness makes man right with God, so they can live. Adam caused many to be sinners because he disobeyed God, and Christ caused many to be made acceptable to God because he obeyed. The Ten Commandments were given so that all could see the extent of their failure to obey God's laws. But the more we see our sinfulness, the more we see God's abounding grace forgiving us.*

Before, sin ruled over all men and brought them to death, but now God's kindness rules instead, giving us right standing with God resulting in eternal life through Jesus Christ our Lord."

What are the limitations of God's forgiveness, how powerful is his love? Perhaps we can get some insight by comparing the questions with an incident recorded in The Living Bible Luke Chapter 5 This incident records some men carrying a paralyzed man on a sleeping mat and lower the paralyzed man down through the roof right in front of Jesus. When Jesus sees their faith he says; (in verse 20*) "My friend your sins are forgiven"* But the religious leaders of the Law call it blasphemy, because who but God can forgive sins (in verse 21) Then Jesus answers in verse 22 *"Why is it blasphemy? I the Messiah, have the authority on earth to forgive sins. But talk is cheap—anybody could say that. So I'll prove it to you by healing this man." Then, turning to the paralyzed men, he commanded, "Pick up your stretcher and go on home, for you are healed!"* Of course the man is immediately healed (verse 25).

Now, keeping this incident in mind, a good question would be, "Is it easier for Jesus to forgive our past sins or our future sins? Can God forgive the future sins we haven't committed yet? The answer is yes. God forgives completely. Sin is simply unbelief; as long as we believe our sins are forgiven, they are. John 16:9 [Jesus says] (TLB), *"The world's sin is unbelief in me."* Please, bear with me, as we take this illustration one step further, to an absolute conclusion by asking, is it easier to forgive the past, future or present sins? Are sins forgiven the moment they are committed? Again the answer is yes. This total forgiveness may seem to some people, as an escape from being accountable for our actions. Strange as it may seem, that's exactly what it is, an escape from being accountable. Jesus paid the price for our actions and our inability to keep from sinning. He became accountable for us. After all we are saved by grace, which is <u>undeserved favor</u>. We humans do not deserve God's love and we never will.

Is it necessary to ask for forgiveness for sins the moment we commit them? Anyone answering yes is living with guilt and not by grace. We can only please God when we live by faith. This means we believe our sins are forgiven unconditionally the moment they are committed. Ephesians 2:4-5 (TLB) *"But God is so rich in mercy; He loved us so much that even though we were spiritually dead and doomed by our sins, He gave us back our lives again when He raised Christ from the dead. Only by his undeserved favor have we ever been saved."*

Years ago, while traveling through Colorado, I noticed some billboard signs along the highway. A farmer, who claimed to be a victim of government rules and regulations, placed these billboards along the highway. One sign in particular stands out in my mind. It said, **"The opposite of freedom is control."** Then I recalled a verse of scripture in John 8:36 (TLB) ***"So if the Son sets you free, you will indeed be free".*** The freedom spoken about, in the Bible, is freedom of all control of our actions, deeds and activities. The only way to experience this freedom is to trust by faith that Jesus has become responsible for our daily actions, deeds and activities. He has already paid the price. Read Jeremiah 39:18 (TLB) *" As a reward for trusting me, I will preserve your life and keep you safe".* Also, Psalms 34:8-10 (TLB), *"Oh, put God to the test and see how kind He is; see for yourself the way His mercies shower down on all who trust Him, if you belong to the Lord reverence* (honor, respect with affections and obey) *Him; for everyone who does this has everything he needs. Even strong young lions go hungry, but those of us who reverence the Lord will never lack any good thing."*

In conclusion of Chapter III, a down-to-earth and apt comparison would be to consider Jesus the **Sun of Man**. Without His light, we would be in total spiritual darkness. In Genesis 1:3 (TLB), *"And God said, Let there be light and there was light."* (Notice the word light is singular.) Verse 4 *"And he saw the light that it was good, and God divided the light from the darkness".* (Notice again light is singular.) This is not only the first act of God, but it also represents Jesus as recorded in John 1:4 (TLB), *In Him was life; and the life was the light of man.* Later, in Genesis 1:14 (TLB) And God said, *"Let there be lights in the firmament of the heaven to divide the day from the night."* Therefore the lights (plural) in Verse 14 are our sun, moon, stars, and other planets.

Chapter 4.

In Chapter III the value of one human soul was emphasized by the Word of God, in Psalms 49:8-9. Can we accept as a fact that one human soul is worth **more** than all of the wealth in, the world? It must be true when we consider the price God paid to save mankind.

Now, a question we might ask is what is so terrible about the lives we live that we should need such an unbelievable valuable sacrifice? Sure, there are a few "bad apples", but the majority of the people appear to be good, honorable, thoughtful and deserving of God's approval. When we evaluate people by their outward appearances, this theory certainly has a lot of credibility.

However, God looks on the inside, of our being, for motives and reasons for our outward actions. 1 Samuel 16:7 (TLB) [the Lord says], ***"I don't make decisions the way you do; man judges by outward appearances, <u>but I look at man's thoughts and intention.</u>"*** Also, King James Bible, Jeremiah 17:10, ***"I, the Lord search the heart, I try the rains even to give every man according to his ways and according to the fruit of his doing."*** The same verse, in the Living Bible, ***Only the Lord knows! He searches all hearts <u>and examines deepest motives</u> so he can give to each person his right reward according to his deeds--how he has lived.***

See, how Jesus explains the inner thoughts of man. Mark 7:20-23 (TLB). ***And he added, "It is the thought life that pollutes. For from within, out of men's hearts, come evil thoughts of lust, theft, murder, adultery, wanting what belongs to others, wickedness, deceit, lewdness, envy, slander, pride and <u>all</u> <u>other folly</u>. All these vile things come from within; they are what pollute you and make you unfit for God."***

The five primary senses of the human soul are imagination, affections, memory, reasoning and conscience. Together, these five senses produce our motives, ambitious desires, intentions and spiritually speaking, ultimately, our beliefs. The human heart, in the spiritual sense, represents the convictions and beliefs of the soul, which produces the fruits (speech) of the soul. ***Whatever is in the heart overflows into speech.*** Luke 6:45 (TLB)

Isn't it strange how our imagination can influence our other senses? For, example, we have all experienced this phenomenal influence, at the theater, while watching a movie. We can be drawn into the plot of the story, being portrayed and begin to associate with the emotions and feeling of the characters the actors are portraying. We know the actors are merely following a script and pretending to be these characters. If we can knowingly be convinced of an illusion, is it plausible that we humans are just naturally acting out a series of different characters throughout our lives? Shakespeare once wrote something to the effect that, "The whole world is a stage and we are actors and actresses, one and all". Perhaps, some people will contend that they are not pretending and insist that life is a serious event and their beliefs will be defended even unto death, if necessary. Well, are not those who profess such beliefs simply serious actors.

At any rate, the Bible explains the condition of the human heart. In the King James Bible, Jeremiah 17:9, ***The heart is deceitful above all things and desperately wicked; who can know it?*** The Living Bible, same passages, says, ***The heart, is the most deceitful thing there is, and desperately wicked. No one can really know how bad it is.*** In this verse of scriptures, God tells us that the human heart is the most deceitful thing there is. It should be emphasized that there is nothing in this world more deceitful then the intentions of the human heart.

Just as an actor or actress can convince an audience that a script is a real event, so we are told that the human heart is far more cunning in fooling us than any performance, the main difference is we are aware of an act, whereas the deceitfulness of the heart, described in the Word of God, can and does fool the world and mankind, as a whole, is the victim.

If no one knows how bad the heart is, how can we humans become aware of its deceitfulness? One source can tell us, Jeremiah 12:10 (TLB*)* ***"Only the Lord knows."*** And, He reveals it to us. Because the fruits (beliefs expressed) of the human heart are the most deceitful and desperately wicked, thing there is, it just naturally and deceitfully minimizes its evil condition to the extent of assuming, believing and even denying that it has an unnatural condition. In fact, the outward appearance and expression indicates that it is basically good. It deceives to the extent of actually appearing sanctimonious.

In a word, what outward appearance fits this description of the desperately wicked human heart perfectly? <u>The answer is religion</u>. Yes, religion all religions of the world are the outward results of the deceitful, desperately wicked human heart expressing its self. Doesn't God describe it as deceitful above all things in the Bible, Jeremiah 17:9? Religion is by the people, of the people, and for the people. Religion deceives people into believing that God has established it and sanctions its activities.

Religion is the outward expression of man trying to appear sanctimonious by a seemingly sacrificial god-like life. It uses deceitful speech, deceitful expressions, deceitful actions and deceitful appearances. Religion deceives by giving the impression that it is grateful, repentant and holy in its actions. It pretends to be pure and sinless in the sight of man and God. It also establishes itself as God's official spokesman.

Let's see what Jesus says about religion in Luke 16:15 (TLB). ***Then He said, "You wear a noble, pious expression in the public, but God knows your evil hearts. Your pretense brings you honor from the people, but it is an abomination in the sight of God".*** Now, let's look at John 12:43 (TLB) ***"for they loved the praise of man more than the praise of God".*** Finally Proverbs 27:21 (TLB), ***"The purity of silver and gold can be tested in a crucible but a man is tested by his reaction to man's praise."***

All, religion is one worldwide cult that deceives by splintering into sects of self, proclaimed individual segments. Each group is duped into believing themselves to be the true followers of God. ***Pretty words may hide wicked heart, just as pretty glaze covers a common clay pot.*** Proverbs 26:23 (TLB). Look at Matthew 15:8-9 (TLB), ***"These people say they honor me but their hearts are far away. Their worship is worthless for they teach their manmade laws instead of those from God."*** Moral ethical and patriotic creeds are good examples of manmade laws.

Contrary to popular beliefs around the world, God does not involve Himself with the activities or situations of man. For example, in the Living Bible, Luke 12:13-14, ***Then someone called from the crowd, "Sir, please tell my brother to divide my father's estate". But Jesus replied, "Man who made me a judge over you to decide such things".*** Also, Ecclesiastes 3:18 (TLB***), And then, I realized that God is letting the world go on its sinful way so that He can test mankind.***

It is a fact that all men are created equal, with certain inalienable faults. Among these faults are **conceit, deceit, contempt and the pursuit of hypocrisy**. In the Oxford American Dictionary the word inalienable is defined as "not able to be given away or taken away". (TLB) Romans3: 10,12 *"As the Scriptures say, "No one is good—no one in all the world is innocent". No one has ever really followed God's paths, or even truly wanted to. Every one has turned away; all have gone wrong. <u>No one anywhere has kept on doing what is right; not one.</u>"*

When did religion begin? Look at Genesis 4:25 (TLB), *Later on Eve gave birth to another son and named him Seth (meaning Granted) for as Eve put it, God has granted me another son for the one Cain killed.* Notice the comment "as Eve put it". This evil sickness becomes generally accepted in verse 26 *When Seth grows up he has a son and named him Enoch. It is during his lifetime that <u>man began to call themselves the Lord's people</u>* (religious). Religion has a form of godliness but denies the miraculous power of God (the purpose and plan of God). Luke 11:52 (TLB), *"Woe to you experts in religion! For you hid the truth from the people, you won't accept it for yourselves, and you prevent others from having a chance to believe it."*

Today in western civilization, an off shoot of religion, the Christianity cult, quotes, teaches and creates its own religion and, like Eve, relegates God to the position of helper. Christianity dupes its followers into accepting themselves as Christ like, people in the image of God. Their church gathering implies that this is the place to worship and learn about God. Like Eve it tries to convince the world that God is associated with its conception and is directly and indirectly responsible for its activities.

Christianity professes a declaration of independence from the world but like a hypocrite it establishes itself as a dictator and authority of the moral standards of the world. Is this Christian image, the same image portrayed by Jesus, while He was living on earth? Quite the contrary, He was an offense to the religious world. In fact, He was so offensive that He was eventually crucified at the prodding of the religious leaders. Matthew 27:1 (TLB), *When it was morning the chief priests and Jewish leaders met again to discuss how to induce the Roman government to sentence Jesus to death.*

See, how Jesus describes religious leaders in Matthew 23:5-10 (TLB), *"Everything they do is done for show. They act holy by wearing on their arms little prayer boxes with scripture* *verses inside, and lengthening the memorial fringes of their robes. And how they love to sit at the head table at banquets and in the reserved pews in the synagogue: How they enjoy the deference paid them on the streets and to be called Rabbi and Master. Don't ever let anyone call you that for only god is your Rabbi and <u>all of you are on the same level,</u> as brothers. <u>And don't address anyone here on earth as Father</u> for only God in heaven should be addressed like that and don't be called Master for only one is your master, even the Messiah."*

Although Jesus is God, He portrayed the image of a common person. For example, notice how He responds to a man's comment in Mark 10:17-19 (TLB), *As he was starting out on a trip, a man came running to him and knelt down and asked, Good teacher, what must I do to get to heaven? <u>Why do you call me good? Jesus asked, Only God is truly good.</u>*

Because there is more insight in Mark (Chapter 10), we should continue with verses 20-27 (TLB), *but as to your question, you know the commandments; don't steal, don't lie, don't cheat, respect your father and mother. Teacher, the man replied, I've never once broken a single one of these laws. Jesus felt genuine love for this man as he looked at him, You lack only one thing, He told him, go and sell all you have and give the money to the poor--and you shall have treasure in heaven--and come follow me. Then the man's face fell, and he went sadly away for he was very rich. Jesus watched him go, then, turned around and said to his disciples, "It's almost impossible for the rich to get into the kingdom of God". This amazed them. So Jesus said it again, "Dear Children how hard it is for those who trust in riches to enter the kingdom of God. It is easier for a camel to go through the eye of a needle than for a rich man to enter the kingdom of God". The disciples were incredulous; "Then who in the world can be saved, if not a rich man?" they asked. Jesus looked at them intently then said, "Without God it is utterly impossible. But with God, everything is possible".* When the man replied, "I've never once broken a single one of these laws," he was revealing his wealth. This testimony was his ticket into the kingdom of God. Jesus was simply telling the man and his disciples that they are not fit for the kingdom of God as long as they are religious.

In chapter II, there was a distinction made between the two natures. The natural and spiritual it was emphasized that the two natures are separate and distinct and should not merge together but this is exactly what religion does, it mixes the condemned natural nature with the spiritual pure nature, thereby polluting the spirit. Galatians 5:19-21 (TLB), ***But when you follow your own wrong instincts (religion), your lives will produce these evil results.***

In Chapter I of this book, page six, the last paragraph explains the first step using faith to establish a relationship with God. An example of this experience is related in the Living Bible and we shall see what happens when faith casts the demon of doubt out of a person. Luke 11:24-26, ***When a demon is cast out of a man, it goes to the deserts, searching there for rest; but finding none it returns to the person it left, and finds that its former home is all swept and clean. Then it goes and gets seven other demons more evil than itself and they all enter the man. And so the poor fellow is seven times worse off then he was before.*** This passage of scripture illustrates what happens when a person first begins by trusting God, by faith, then turns into a religious fanatic. Some examples of these demons are -- one demon convinces this poor fellow that he is now levitated above the dirty earth and the dirty people. Another convinces this poor fellow that he is now able to purify mankind. The third demon convinces this poor fellow that he is a righteous judge of the morals and ethics of other people. The fourth demon turns this poor fellow into a condemning judge. Another demon has this poor fellow quoting scripture verses. Another demon causes this poor fellow to yell and scream at people trying to scare them into becoming religious. Another demon puts this poor fellow in a position that allows him to excommunicate anyone that does not agree with his creeds. The seventh demon convinces this poor fellow that he is obligated to follow the precepts of the religious world he now lives in. Jeremiah 17:5 (TLB), ***The Lord says cursed is the man who puts his trust in mortal man and turns his heart away from God***.

Chapter 5

According to the American Heritage Dictionary Religion is! 1(a) "An organized system of beliefs and rituals centering on a supernatural being or beings. (b) Adherence to such a system. 2. A belief upheld or pursued with zeal and devotion." Religious is! 1. "Of or relating to religion. 2. Adhering to or manifesting religion; pious; godly. 3. Scrupulous, conscientious. 4. Of or belonging to a monastic order, (pl.ious). A person belonging to a monastic order, as a monk or nun."

How can I be so critical of religion? Is it possible that I have a personal vendetta against religion? Yes I must admit, I hate religion, however, it wasn't always like this. About 30 years ago I became totally engrossed in religion. This total commitment kept me busy doing my best to follow all the precepts I was taught and reasoned, necessary to fulfill the spiritual laws of my chosen religion. I must admit I was very naïve, taking it all very serious, striving for perfection.

I recall one instance, for example, while visiting a friend, I noticed a few granules of, what appeared to be, either salt or sugar on the tablecloth so wetting my finger I touched the substance and tasted it. It was salt, and the moment I tasted it a wave of guilt swept over me because I had actually stolen the grains of salt from this friend. Why be so "nit picking" you may ask? "Well" my answer is, "who draws the line between right and wrong?" "How does any one know for sure?" If you're trying to keep God's laws then a few grains of salt taken from another person's table is stealing, pure and simple.

These fanatical religious antics burdened me with a constant load of guilt. Eventually a few passages of scripture were revealed to me. This revelation was not a booming voice from heaven. It was more like a piece of the puzzle coming together. This revelation allowed me to understand that my relationship with God in not contingent upon my being good but by believing in God's promises of forgiveness.

The scripture verses that were revealed are as follows. In the King James Bible the book of Galatians chapter 3 starting with verse 2 ***"This only would I learn from you, Received ye the Spirit by the works of the law, or by the hearing of faith. Are ye so foolish? Having began in the Spirit are ye now made perfect by the flesh".***

I had started my relationship with God, by simply believing in Him, and then my natural senses (flesh) of reasoning and imagination convince me that I should change my ways in order to prove that I was a new person. However, because I am an imperfect human being I found myself, constantly failing to fulfill the image my religion demanded. As a result I was constantly under God's curse. Continuing Galatians 3 verse 4 ***"Have ye suffered so many things in vain? If it be*** *yet in vain. (5) He therefore that ministrereth to you the Spirit, and worketh miracles among ye, doeth he it by the works of the law, or by the hearing of faith? (6) Even as Abraham believed God and it was accounted to him for righteousness."*

Even the apostle Paul, who wrote the book of Galatians, testifies about coming to the same conclusion that I had come to. Quoting the Apostle Paul in Galatians 2:19 (The Living Bible) *"for it was through reading the Scripture that I came to realize I could never find God's favor by trying- and failing- to obey the laws. I came to realize that acceptance with God comes by believing in Christ."*

Religion, on the other hand, relies on outward appearance and outward actions it never relies on faith. Religion doesn't believe in faith it tries to control the evil nature and direct it's path by (pious) natural activities.

I could go on explaining and giving more examples of the fallacy of religion but may not be any more convincing. The results of an experience may speak volumes. Jesus said in the book of John chapter 14 verse 12 (King James Bible) *"verily, verily, I say unto you He that believeth on me the works that I do shall he do also; and greater works than these shall he do; because I go unto my Father".*

In my case, the greater works, spoken about in this verse of scripture, is my experience of being delivered from religion. It is hard to describe the utter relief and exuberant joy I felt when I began to believe and accept God's sacrifice as payment for my faulty life. Here is a fact in my life, and is also my eternal creed, "I could not know Jesus as a personal friend until I had denounced religion in my life."

Psalms 40 verse 2 (King James Bible) *"He brought me also up out of an horrible pit, out of the miry clay, and set my feet upon a rock and established my goings".* Is it probable, that many people would consider this verse of scripture a hypothetical experience or perhaps the description of a dream or nightmare? On the other hand it describes very clearly my feeling while in the pit of miry religion, even though I was not fully aware of the horror I was experiencing until after God had miraculously brought me out of that horrible pit. Because of this wonderful spiritual healing I have developed an eternal respect and a deep reverence for God. Psalms 25:4 (TLB) *"Friendship with God is reserved for those who reverence Him. With them alone He shares the secrets of his promises."*

The real war, of life, is taking place in the spiritual dimension. Ephesians 6:13 (TLB) *"For we are not fighting against people made of flesh and blood, but against persons without bodies---the evil rulers of the unseen world, those mighty satanic beings and great evil princes of darkness who rule this world; and against huge numbers of wicked spirits in the sprit world."* If we accept as fact that "the evil princes of darkness rule this world" it's easy to visualize religion as the stronghold of the satanic regime. Spiritually speaking, when a person becomes religious, this individual becomes a citizen of the satanic regime. These people began to break the spiritual laws of god. Think about this, the first of the Ten Commandments is *"Thou shalt have no other god's before me"* (Exodus chapter 20 verse 3 King James Bible) When a person becomes religious, the religion becomes the most important thing in this persons life. Religion becomes this person's god thereby breaking the first commandment.

The second commandment (verse 4) is *"thou shalt not make unto thee any graven image, or any likeness of anything that is in the heaven above, or that is in the earth beneath, or that is in the water under the earth,"* Again when a person becomes religious this person presents a religious image to the world. This image is the likeness of a pious person. This self created image breaks the second commandment.

The third commandment is *"thou shalt not bow down thyself to them, nor serve them: for I the Lord thy God am a jealous God."* (verse 5 KJ) When a person becomes religious this person will bow down to all the precepts and serve the religion. This person will also praise the other members of the sect and accept praise from others. Exalting of each other breaks the third commandment.

(Verse 7 KJ) *"Thou shalt not take the name of the Lord thy God in vain; for the Lord will not hold him guiltless that taketh his name in vain."* We human beings are under a curse as a result of our ancestors, Adam and Eve, disobeying God. When a person uses the comment "God bless you" this person is using the Lords name in vain. This comment, along with other religious comments, is giving a false message and contradicts the curse thereby refusing to reverence God's word.

(Verse 8 KJ) **Remember the Sabbath day, to keep it holy.** Actually Jesus fulfilled all of the commandments, including observing the Sabbath. Religions observing the "literal" Sabbath are denying the Sacrifice. In fact, according to God's word, when Jesus died on the cross, He fulfilled God's purpose and we are instructed to observe the Sabbath by entering into His place of rest. This place of rest is a permanent condition of the soul. This means simply to stop being religious by observing special days or events. A person cannot exert effort by observing these special days and cease from all activities at the same time. We are destined to do one or the other. Hebrews 4:9-12 (TLB) *"So there is a full complete rest still waiting for the people of God. Christ has already entered there. He is resting from his work, just as God did after the Creation. Let us do our best to go into that place of rest too being careful not to disobey God as the children of Israel did, thus failing to get in. <u>For whatever God says is full of living power.</u>"* Colossians 2:16&17 (TLB) *"So don't let anyone criticize for what you eat or drink or for not celebrating Jewish holidays and feasts or new moon ceremonies or <u>Sabbaths</u> for these were only temporary rules that ended when Christ came. They were only shadows of the real thing---of Christ himself."*

(Verse 12 KJ) **Honor thy father and thy mother---** Spiritually, speaking God is our father and Jesus is our mother. God became our spiritual father when he planted the holy seed in the Virgin Mary, which resulted in the birth of Jesus. When Jesus died on the cross his death gave birth to all who believe, his spiritual children, God's real offspring. Religions of the world interpret this commandment to mean our earthly parents thus failing to Honor the real father and mother.

Exodus 20:13 (KJ) **Thou shalt not kill--** When a person becomes religious this person begins to kill (spiritually) other people. A religious person is sending a message to the world that their religion has given them life and those who don't have their religious beliefs are doomed. They kill by condemning unreligious people. James 5:6 (TLB) *"You have condemned and killed good men who had no power to defend themselves against you"*.

(Verse 14 KJ) ***Thou shalt not commit adultery--*** Most people consider this commandment an earthly event between a husband and wife. However spiritually speaking this is strictly a relationship between religious people and God. Read Isaiah 54:5 (TLB) ***"---for your creator will be your "husband"----.*** Is this verse just idle chatter? Is it just a figure of speech? Is God speaking to someone in past history? Or are these words, also for us? Now read Isaiah 57:7&8 (TLB) ***"You have committed adultery on the tops of the mountains, for you worship idols there deserting me. Behind closed doors you set your idols up and worship someone other than me. This is adultery for you are giving these idols your love, instead of loving me".*** Religious people love their religion and worship their religion. A person's religion is their idol. This is breaking God's commandment "thou shalt not commit adultery".

Exodus 20:15 (KJ) ***Thou shalt not steal--***The divinity of Christ is stolen by religion pretending to be the divine incarnation of God.

Exodus 20:16 (KJ) ***Thou shalt not bear false witness against thy neighbor--*** Jesus is our neighbor, because he lives in our heart. Jesus died on the cross to deliver us from our sinful nature (the natural man) Religion tries to make us believe that God is trying to repair the "natural man" which is deceiving and presenting a false witness against our Savior.

Exodus 20:17 (KJ) ***"Thou shalt not covet thy neighbor's house, thou shalt not covet thy neighbors wife, nor his man servant, nor his maid servant, nor his ox, nor his ass, nor anything that is thy neighbor.".*** Religions covet, the unseen spiritual house of our neighbor Jesus, by erecting man made houses of worship. In fact the very nature of religion is to covet everything that belongs to Jesus. There you have it; the Ten Commandments are all broken by religion. Psalms 73:20 (TLB) ***"Their present life is only a dream! They will awaken to the truth as one awakens from a dream of things that never really were!"*** Perhaps now is the time to talk about the greatest of all commandments. In the Living Bible Jesus explains Mark 12:29-31 (TLB)***"Hear O Israel The Lord our God is the one and only God. And you must love him with all your heart and soul and mind and strength. The second is: You must love others as much as yourself. No other commandments are greater than these."*** So how can a person love God this much? Of course, to love somebody you must first know the person and develop trust, honor, respect, and have a desire to be close to the person and probably most of all you must be compatible.

The bible declares, "God is love". No wonder the greatest commandment of all is to love God with all our heart, soul, strength and mind. How does a person know how much they love God? Jesus has an experience, which gives an example, of complete love and partial love. Saint Luke chapter 7 verses 36 through 46 King James Bible. The 47th verse has the nugget of truth, that gives the formula for complete love and partial love and I quote: *"Wherefore I say unto thee, her sins, which are many, are forgiven: for she loved much: but to whom little is forgiven, the same loveth little."* Keeping this verse of scripture in mind, we need to truthfully ask ourselves, how much sin do I have today that I hope is forgiven? One thing is certain; religious people appear to have fewer sins than nonreligious people. Therefore, nonreligious people seeking forgiveness will naturally love more. If I am hopelessly deadlocked in sin, if my very nature is pure sin, then I am in an excellent position to love God with all my heart, soul mind and strength because He simply forgives me in spite of my corrupt condition.

With all this forgiveness we could easily love God with all our heart, soul, mind and strength. The result is total compatibility. **Could we with ink the ocean fill, And were the skies of parchment made, Were every stock on earth a quill And every man a scribe by trade, To write the love of God above Would drain the ocean dry, Nor could the scroll contain the whole Tho stretched from sky to sky.** These words were found scrawled on the wall of a cell in a mental ward, and has become the third verse of the song **The Love Of God**.

A popular song often sung at funerals is **Amazing Grace** but this song was written by somebody while they were alive, for the living, and should be a constant theme in our hearts. As we know grace means <u>undeserved favor</u>. **"Amazing grace (undeserved favor) how sweet the sound that saved a wretch like me! I once was lost but now am found, was blind but now I see. Twas grace (undeserved favor) that taught my heart to fear, and grace (undeserved favor) my fears relieved; how precious did that grace (underserved favor) appear the hour I first believed."**

The second greatest commandment is-- *"you must love others as much as yourself No other commandments are greater than these".* Mark 12:31 (TLB). How can we know if we love others as much as ourselves? Romans 13:9&10 (TLB) *"If you love others as much as you love yourself you will not want to harm or cheat him or kill him or steal from him. And you won't sin with his wife or want what is his, or do anything else the Ten Commandments say is wrong. All ten are wrapped up in this one, to love your neighbor as you love yourself."* As was pointed out earlier, in this chapter, religious people break the Ten Commandments.

The only way to show true love to your fellow man is to eradicate religion from your life. It's ironic that the verse of scripture that proves this point is a mirror of one quoted previously in this book namely John 3:16. Now look at 1 John 3:16 (TLB) *"We know what real love is from Christ's example in dying for us. And so we also ought to lay down our lives for our Christian brothers."* Only by sacrificing our religious ties can we stop condemning our fellow man. If we have no religion we won't look down on others.

As The Apostil Paul points out in Galatians 5:24 (TLB) *"Those who belong to Christ have nailed their natural evil (religious) desires to his cross and crucified them there."* Am I injecting my own thought into this verse? Look at Colossians 3:3 (TLB) *"You should have as little desire for this world as a dead person does"* ----

God speaks to us, vicariously, every night as we sleep. Aren't all our daily activities abandoned and unimportant while we are asleep? Isn't the message being impressed upon us that our experiences here on earth are just the shadows of life. Philippians 3:7 (TLB) *"But all these things that I once thought worthwhile now I've thrown them all away so I can put my trust and hope in Christ alone. Yes everything else is worthless when compared with the priceless gain of knowing Christ Jesus my Lord. I have put aside all else, counting it worth less than nothing, in order that I can have Christ, and become one with him, no longer counting on being saved <u>by being good enough</u> or by obeying God's laws<u>, but by trusting Christ</u> to save me; for God's way of making us right with him <u>depends on faith</u>---counting on Christ <u>alone</u>. Now I* *have given up everything else---I have found it to be the only way to really know Christ and experience the mighty power that brought him back to life again---,"*

The Bible declares God is a trinity---Father, Son and Holy Spirit. I recall an Atheist program on T.V. The host asked, defiantly, "How can God be three separate parts and claim to be one? First of all if were inquiring with an inquisitive attitude we would assuredly get an answer. However if we're trying to establish doubt in God we will never get an answer. If we really believe in God our first thought tells us we can never limit God or doubt what He says. God is spirit and is therefore omnipresent. The answer to this question is within us. We humans are three in one, body, soul and spirit. Because religion is distorted and merges the soul and spirit, it assumes the soul and spirit are the same, and is therefore unable and unwilling to conceive of these two separate parts of the human being. The human body's five main senses are sight, smell, feel, taste and hear the five main senses of the soul are imagination, affections, memory, reasoning and conscience the five main senses of the spirit are love, joy, peace, faith and hope. So we can perceive of God as three in one as we are made of three in one.

The reason for bringing up this subject, about the concept of three separate parts in one body is to explain about a spiritual surgery to separate the human soul from the spirit. The human soul is contaminated and evil through and through if we can accept this truth we will be willing to sacrifice the religious activities (fruits) of the soul.

For me this experience was a broken heart and a broken spirit. As I recall, it was a real heart-wrenching event, it was my deepest feeling of remorse, a complete sense of helplessness and utter regret for my souls evil condition. I was in a deep remorseful condition, for about a week, with uncontrollable excruciating regret, as I experienced the demise, of religion in my life. James 4:9&10 (TLB) *"Let there be tears for the wrong things you have done. Let there be sorrow and sincere grief. Let there be sadness instead of laughter, and gloom instead of joy. <u>Then when you realize your worthlessness before the Lord, he will lift you up, encourage and help you.</u>"*

Psalms 51:17 (KJ) *"The sacrifices of God are a broken spirit a broken and contrite heart, O God, thou wilt not despise."* Psalms 34:18 (KJ) *"The Lord is nigh unto them that are of a broken heart; and saveth such as be of a contrite spirit.* Isaiah 66:1 (TLB) *"Heaven is my throne and the earth is my footstool: What Temple can you build for me as good as that? My hand has made both earth and skies and they are mine. Yet I will look down with pity on the man who has a humble and a contrite heart, <u>who trembles at my word</u>.* Isaiah 57:15 (KJ) *"For thus saith the high and lofty One that inhabiteth eternity, whose name is Holy; I dwell in the high and holy place, with him also that is of a contrite and humble spirit<u>, to revive the spirit of the humble, and to revive the heart of the contrite ones.</u>"* When I first became religious I had "found my life" (so to speak) later on I gave up the religious life. St. Mathew 10:39 (KJ) *"He that findeth his life shall lose it: and he that loseth his life for my sake shall find it."* This verse simply means we will eventually lose our religion, but if we willingly give it up, for his sake we will find real life.

My outward appearance is strictly natural and has no apparent connection with the spiritual life that I've been talking about. Those who know me are, for the most part, are unaware of my connection with God. So this may appear that I am hiding my beliefs and am ashamed of my faith in God but this is part of the suffering that spiritual people experience. God is my judge and as long as I satisfy Him that is all that matters.

Although I no longer cherish religion I do not advocate the overthrow or condone terrorist attacks against religion. Being dead (spiritually) to this world I have no moral, ethical or religious cause to fight for. I am not trying to start another church or religion. Like our spiritual father Abraham I'm a pilgrim and a stranger here on earth. Hebrews 11:8,9&10 (TLB) *"Abraham trusted God, and when God told him to leave home and go far away to another land, which he promised to give him, Abraham obeyed. Away he went, not even knowing where he was going. And even when he reached God's promised land<u>, he lived in tents like a mere visitor</u>, as did Isaac and Jacob, to whom God gave the same promise. Abraham did this because he was confidently waiting for God to bring him to that strong heavenly city whose designer and builder is God".*

Psalms 73:28 (TLB) *"But as for me, I get as close to him as I can! I have chosen him and I will tell everyone about the wonderful ways he rescues me."* Isaiah 57 (TLB) *"The good men perish; the godly die before their time and no one seems to care or wonder why. No one seems to realize that God is taking them away from evil days ahead. For the godly who die shall rest in peace".* This verse is not talking about a physical death but rather the spiritual death of earthly moral, ethical and religious creeds. Spiritual people are dead to this world and are citizens, vicariously, of God's spiritual kingdom; this condition is as distinct from night and day as the natural world is distinct from the spiritual world. Ephesians 2:19 (KJ) *"Now therefore ye are no more strangers and foreigners, but fellow citizens with the saints, and are the household of God."* Psalms 73:24 (TLB) *"you will keep on guiding me all my life with your wisdom and counsel; and afterwards receive me into the glories of heaven! Whom have I in heaven but you? And I desire no one on earth as much as you! My health fails; my spirits droop, yet God remains! He is the strength of my heart; He is mine forever!"*

Chapter 6

Approximately 12 years ago (would be 1993) my youngest son said to me "Dad, people down through history, who have had something important to say recorded the information for future generations and you have something important to say". It was at this time that I started writing this book. From the beginning I planed for chapter five to be the last chapter. A few people have been receiving the chapters, as they were completed. Among these people is my sister Gail. After receiving chapter 5, Gail's reply was **"Looking forward to next chapter, but take your time- theirs a well of information inside of you- but let it work it's way out naturally"** Gail's comment has become my motivation and encouragement to continue writing. Thus chapter 6 is born.

Throughout this book, all of the examples, conclusions, and comments have been the result of obvious reasoning with occasional trivial comments. For this reason the fundamental understanding of God is available to all mankind regardless of intellectual or cultural differences. For example in Chapter 1 there is a quote from Professor Hawkins's book, titled "A brief history of time" the quote implies his belief in God. At the time of this writing, Professor Hawking is the Professor of Mathematics at the University of Cambridge in England. On the other end of the scale there is a quote in chapter 5 of a profound description of God's love scrawled on the wall of a mental ward, which also implies a belief in God. Keeping these thoughts in mind we may reason "the third most important event in life is becoming aware of the obvious. The second most important event in life is realizing the importance of discovering the obvious. And the single most important event in life is to embrace the obvious as though it were the very essence of life. Now if we substitute the word obvious with the word God it will become clear that the two words are synonymous. In the Bible and the book of Acts chapter 26, there is an example of this obvious trivial reasoning as Paul is defending his faith in the prophecies of Jesus Christ, by using apparent trivial examples of his experiences. Notice how King Agrippa replies. In verse 28 (TLB) ***Agrippa interrupted him. "With trivial proofs like these, you expect me to become a Christian?"***

One of the main themes of this book has been to distinguish and separate the natural human nature and the natural world from the spiritual nature and the spiritual world. The natural human nature is permanently endowed with a doubtful existence and a negative attitude towards God. The natural human nature is destined to pretend that life on earth is real. Man does this by acting out and creating an illusion of life. This illusion is manifested as religious and political themes. The activities of religion and political themes are based on outward expressions, opinions, theories and distorted beliefs. Distorted because these beliefs are a desperate attempt to correct, control and present a false illusion of man evolving into loving, caring people. The past history of man, and present events, indicates that we are moving towards a "de-evolving" condition. In other words man is on a path of self-destruction. Most of us have thought, to ourselves, or heard people say "I don't want to bring children into this world". Why would a person come to this conclusion? It's because of the trauma of coping with a chaotic nature. Not only are we subjected to natural uncertainties of nature but the out of control fascist governments and a whole spectrum of individual human perversions are common events. It should be noted here that all human beings, to one degree or another, are included in this spectrum of human perversions. Although we as individuals may not be outwardly responsible for these perversions there is an inborn tendency for each individual to act out these perversions. Just the day-by-day problems, pressures, pain and suffering are signs of a perverted human nature.

What appears to be normal and natural to mankind is our acceptance of this chaotic condition. It's like we cherish the opportunity to overcome and force our environment to succumb to our wants and needs. This attitude produces pride in our lives, religions, and governments. Pride is a dangerous trap that renders a person deaf and blind to common sense. Pride fools a person into feeling compatible with the natural environment and is mistaken for wisdom, intelligence and spirituality. Pride blinds a person from seeing our chaotic condition. Pride is the riches (hypocrisy) of the world and is cherished by those who posses it and loathed by those who have discarded it. Proverbs 8:13 (TLB) *If anyone respects and fears God, he will hate evil. For <u>wisdom</u> <u>hates pride</u>, arrogance, corruption and deceit of every kind.* Proverbs 16:5 (TLB) *Pride disgusts the Lord. Take my word for it---proud men shall be punished.* The same verse King James Bible "*Every one that is proud in heart is an abomination to the Lord: though hand joins hand, he shall not be unpunished.* Proverbs 16:18 (TLB) "*Pride goes before destruction and haughtiness before a fall*". Of course, all religions of the world are included in this prediction. A couple of examples of prideful people, in the world at the time of this writing, would be Pope John Paul II and Osama bin Laden. These men and their followers are full of pride. John 12:43 (TLB) *for they loved the praise of man more than the praise of God.* Isaiah 2:22 (TLB) *Puny man! Frail as his breath! Don't ever put your trust in him!* To the world Jeffrey Dahmer, a serial killer, is an example of evil in its purest form. However, unlike Pope John Paul II and Osama bin Laden. Jeffrey Dahmer was punished here on earth and there was no indication that he was proud of his actions or life style.

For the most part, mankind regards the spiritual world as an illusion or a figment of our imagination. The natural world and man are looked upon as an end in itself and appears to have all the necessary ingredients of reality. In actuality the natural world and all the man made societies are illusions and the spiritual world is pure reality, which can be perceived by using our God given gift of faith. In chapter one, you may recall, faith is the substance and evidence of things unseen (the spiritual world). Hebrews 11:1 (TLB) *What is faith? It is the confident assurance that something we want is going to happen. It is the certainty that what we hope for is waiting for us, even though we cannot see it up ahead.* Notice in this verse of scripture it is what we hope for, though we cannot see it up ahead. What God is saying is that faith is not a physical outward visible experience but an inward unseen belief.

Those people who agree with the information presented in this manuscript know, that in reality, there is only one God and He is the creator of all things. First Corinthians 8:6 (TLB*) "But we know that there is only one God, the Father, who created all things and made us to be his own; and one Lord Jesus Christ, who made everything and gives us life."*

Satan the Devil is a phony god and all his attributes are strictly false. Satan is the god of illusion and of the natural world. He appears to have creative abilities but they are always phony. An illusion is actually a lie because it appears to be real but is not. We are children of a fallen, corrupt nature; from our birth to death we human beings live a lie. Because of this distortion we mistakenly perceive this earthly life as real with the illusion that we can have a normal life on earth. Our human ambitions, desires and goals are all illusions. Your opinion and my opinion are just illusions. Ecclesiasstes12: 12 (TLB) ***But, my son, be warned: there is no end of opinions ready to be expressed....*** The existence we experience here on earth is an illusion. To prove these points just ask yourself "what ambitions, desires, goals, religious or political beliefs and any other aspect of life am I concerned about while I'm sleeping?" The answer is none of the above. Therefore the message being impressed upon us daily throughout our lives, as we sleep, is that "life on earth is not real it's an illusion". Job 33:14&15 (TLB) ***"For God speaks again and again, in dreams, in visions of the night when deep sleep falls on men as they lie on their beds.***

For those people trying to improve the condition of mankind or live a pious lifestyle their will be a rude awakening, when this life is over, they will discover that it was all for nothing, just an illusion. The only reward for these "life stylist" is self-pride and an illusive memory. Both will end in bitter regret. Psalms 73:20(TLB) ***"Their present life is only a dream! They will awaken to the truth as one awakens from a dream of things that never really were!***

As a general rule man believes that religion is synonymous with a belief in God. "If you're not religious you don't believe in God." This is a good example of an illusion that is perpetrated by Satan and accepted by the general population. Actually religious people are the one's who don't believe in God. Yes, they believe that there is a God but so do the satanic demons. James 2:19 (TLB) ***"Are there still some among you who hold that "only believing" is enough? Believing in one God? Well, remember that the demons believe this too---so strongly that they tremble in terror!*** Strange as it may seem religion is what keeps a person from believing in God. The simple fact is that religion is an outward expression of a distorted belief, while a spiritual belief is an inward expression. Religion presents a false image to the world it pretends to be pious but this image is a satanic trick. Here it is forks the unquestionable proof that our strength is from within. Ephesians 6:10 (TLB) ***Last of all I want to remind you that your strength must come from the Lord's mighty power <u>within you</u>. Put on all of God's armor so that you will be able to stand safe against all strategies and tricks of Satan.*** How do I know this statement is true? I have personally experienced this phenomenon. I was religious at one time in my life and am now not religious. For me being non-religious is better because I quit pretending and actually began to believe. Here's more proof that Satan controls this religious and political world. Ephesians 6:12

(TLB) *For we are not fighting against people made of flesh and blood, but against persons without bodies—the evil rulers of the unseen world, those mighty satanic beings and great evil princes of darkness <u>who rule this world</u>; and against huge numbers of wicked spirits in the spirit world.* 1st John 5:19 (TLB) *We know that we are children of God and that <u>all the rest of the world around us is under Satan's power and control.</u>* The controversial aspect of this condition is that anybody who is truly spiritual will not appear to have any outward expressions of their belief. We just go about our daily lives as just another abnormal filthy human being. For example I enjoy watching the Jerry Springer and Howard Stern TV shows. Often when I am angry or frustrated I express my feelings with profanity. I enjoy all types of "so called" evil worldly entertainment even x rated entertainment I will never be a part of, or watch, the 700 club, Billy Graham crusades or any other religious program on TV or radio.

I realize that you who are reading this book will have your own ideas about our destiny. However, we cannot clam ignorance of the information presented. Each person has a choice to confirm this philosophy of life by checking scripture to prove this information true. (Acts 17-11 (TLB) ---*They searched the Scriptures day by day to check up on Paul and Silas statements to see if they were really so.* Or you can prove the information untrue by looking for ways to establish doubt that will allow you to reject this philosophy of life. Proverbs11: 27 (TLB) *If you search for good you will find God's favor; if you search for evil you will find his curse*. The third option is, not to accept or reject this philosophy of life but to simply ignore the information presented. 2 Corinthians 6:9 (TLB) *"The world ignores us,----*

What about prayer? Does a contaminated nature (man) know how to pray to a perfect God? The answer is no. Those who pray before meals, at bedtime, and in their religious gatherings are proving they don't really know God. It's simple to explain, when a person prays out loud they are proving that God is not part of their life. They are showing by this outward action that God is out their somewhere in the cosmos. If God is in our heart we commute internally, in our spirit, with emotions of gratitude, grace, love, and adoration for His perfect gift of life. Romans 8:26-27 (TLB) *And in the same way—by our faith—the Holy Spirit helps us with our daily problems and in our praying. For <u>we don't even know what we should pray for</u>, <u>nor how to pray as we should</u>; but the Holly Spirit prays for us <u>with such feeling that it cannot be expressed in words.</u> And the Father who knows all hearts knows, of course, what the Spirit is saying as he pleads for us in harmony with God's own will.*

Many years ago I recall looking through my bedroom window, on a clear night. As I gazed into the havens I asked God if I could shine, in his kingdom, as the brightness of a star that I was looking at. It wasn't the brightest star in the universe. But, from my vantage point it was the brightest star I could see. I believe the information presented in this manuscript is a result of this prayer and has been revealed to me by God's spirit and I am convinced that it is the true Gospel (good news) being offered to anybody willing to consider its validity. 1 Corinthians 2:16 (TLB)-- --***But, strange as it seems, we Christians actually do have within us a portion of the very thoughts and mind of Christ.*** I also recall another experience, many years ago, while waiting for a sandwich, I had ordered, at a fast food restaurant. A well dressed business man, a stranger, sitting next to me, made a comment he said **" I envy you"** unfortunately I didn't question his comment and their was nothing else said between us. At the time I did not know why he made this statement, later I found a verse of scripture, which confirmed what the stranger was conveying to me. Romans 4:7 (TLB)***"Blessed, and to be envied,"*** he said, ***"are those whose sins are forgiven and put out of sight. "Yes, what joy there is for anyone whose sins are no longer counted against him by the Lord."***

Recently, in December 2004, there was a Tsunami that mostly devastated the coast of Indonesia, Sri Lauka and India causing loss of life, over 100,000 people died, and catastrophic destruction. Why would God allow such a catastrophe to occur? Isn't the message to the world and mankind that life here on earth is a temporary and unstable? Shouldn't this cause us to want to become aware of, and search for the obvious gift of life? Probably the most obvious observation of all is the total and complete denial of man to accept God's plan and purpose of redemption. <u>He simply wants somebody to fall in love with Him and begin to really appreciate what He has done to accomplish this end result.</u> We live in a contaminated world with the Devil as our god and this is why the human race is unable to save itself and every effort to do so confirms the previous observation of denial. James 4:10 (TLB) ***Then when you realize your worthlessness (attitude) before the lord, he will lift you up, encourage and help you.*** Years ago I wrote the lyrics to a song and would like to share these words with those who are searching for answers and would like to express their appreciation to Jesus for making it possible to have eternal life. **"There are tears of joy and gain, there are tears of sad refrain there are tears when those we've known have passed away. There are tears that flow like rain when we have despairing pain but the most precious tears of all are the tears that rarely flow and they are the tears of gratitude.**

Tears of gratitude, tears of gratitude like pure droplets of crystal in His sight Jesus died now all will live nothing good have we to give so I'll gladly shed these tears of gratitude. Tears of gratitude tears of gratitude like pure droplets of crystal in His sight tears like rivers on the land flowing down the face of man but tell me where are the tears of gratitude?"

In recent times, a correspondent brought a scripture to my attention and commented on it.Matthew 5:5 (King James Bible) *blessed are the meek: for they shall inherit the earth*. He said, "I totally reject the Christian teachings. I was raised to believe so I did. But once I studied Christianity I came to realize that the Christian teachings are in total conflict with the laws of nature. I believe Christianity has done way more harm than good. It is a religion for the weak and downtrodden, the meek and slaves. History shows that the meek will not inherit the earth, but the strong will as they always have. If you love your enemy they will destroy you." Of course I agree with this logic. If we interpret this scripture into the natural world it is unquestionably true. However if we interpret it spiritually and it fits into God's spiritual realm it can and does make sense. Consider this thought, who is your enemy? Do you really know who your enemy is? If you want to see your enemy take a look in the mirror. Our inner being, the soul is the companion that we are associated with while we exist on earth. The soul can and does establish our life long beliefs, whether true or false Psalms55: 12 (TLB) *It was not an enemy who taunted me—then I could have born it; I could have hidden and escaped. But it was you, a man like myself, my companion and my friend. What fellowship we had, what wonderful discussions as we walked together to the Temple of the Lord on holy days.* The earth to be inherited is your, inner self, your own earthly body. Think about it, our earthly life is each persons "whole world" When we realize that it's what we believe and our attitude that control our destiny and we take steps to change them we can truly "inherit" our world. I know because I have inherited my world. Another word to describe it is called "salvation" That is saved from our, inner, natural distorted beliefs and evil attitude, of our soul, and the distorted beliefs and teachings of the world. Isaiah 57: 12 (TLB) *...But he who trusts in me shall possess the land and inherit my Holy Mountain.*

Are you one of the many people who believe that God is directing your earthly life day by day? Do you feel that each experience in your life is part of His plan? If we analyze this theory with an inquisitive attitude it will allow some spiritual light to shine on the subject. First of all we live in a changing world that is always threatened with chaotic episodes. One example is the Tsunami previously mentioned where over 100,000 people lost their lives. Does it make sense that God would protect a few religious people and allow the rest of humanity to be subjected to the unpredictable catastrophic events that happen? Isn't it logical to conclude that a few of the 100,000 people who died in the Tsunami, believed that God was "divinely" protecting them? God is no respecter of persons. Romans 2:11 (TLB) *For God treats everyone the same.* Nobody on earth is being "divinely" protected and yes, God does make junk if we weren't junk we wouldn't be deteriorating into oblivion. Romans 9:22 (TLB) *Does not God have a perfect right to show his fury and power against those who are fit only for destruction, those he has been patient with for all this time?* Consider this, we live in a ever changing world, God never changes, we live in a chaotic world, God is perfect, this world is temporary, God is eternal, this natural world is scheduled for a huge bonfire, God is a consuming fire 2 Peter 3:10 *The day of the Lord is surely coming, as unexpectedly as a thief, and then the heavens will pass away with a terrible noise and the heavenly bodies will disappear in fire and the earth and everything on it will be burned up*. Do you recall what Jesus said before He was crucified? John 18:36 (TLB) *Then Jesus answered, "I am not on earthly king. If I were, my followers would have fought when I was arrested by the Jewish leaders. But my Kingdom is not of the world."* Doesn't this comment indicate that there are two worlds? Check this out in John 15:19 (TLB) *The world would love you if you belonged to it, but you don't—for I chose you to come out of the world, and so it hates you. John 17:15 (TLB) I'm not asking you to take them out of the world, but to keep them safe from Satan's power (*false beliefs*) They are not part of this world any more than I am.*

The ultimate triumph in our natural life is to die out to political and religious beliefs of the world and accept our existence on earth as one continuous filthy, corrupt event. This condition implies that one does not become involved with worldly issues. Colossians 2:3 (TLB) mentioned in chapter 5 *You should have as little desire for this world as a dead person does.* Does a dead person debate popular issues of the day? Do the people buried in the cemetery care who are right or wrong? Is the dead trying to improve world conditions? Do the dead care about your political or religious views? Do they care whither or not you bring flowers to their grave? If I die out to this world how can I have a voice on controversial subjects that affect my earthly life? If I did then I would be a hypocrite. The only good thing anybody can do is admit to this chaotic, distorted condition and rely past, present and future on God's mercy and rejoice in the ultimate sacrifice namely Jesus the only one who managed to live a perfect life. Psalms 17:15 (TLB) *But as for me my contentment is not in wealth* (pies religious or political life) *but in seeing you and knowing all is well between us and when I awake in heaven I will be fully satisfied for I will see you face to face.*

Merrily, merrily, merrily, merrily (this natural) life is but a dream.

Chapter 7

After receiving chapter 6 of this book, my sister Gail asked if their would be any more chapters and I said chapter 6 would be the last chapter. Of course I pondered this comment and began to realize there is **"life after religion"** therefore, chapter 7 is a **"rebirth chapter."**

While contemplating chapter 7, it dawned on me that at the beginning of chapter 6, I indicated to my sister that chapter 5 was, what I had planned to be the last chapter of this book. Then I went on to explain how my sister's comment had inspired me to continue with chapter 6. Since I had not planned chapter 6 it has occurred to me that I am being enlightened at the same time this information is being recorded. It's like the information is in my spirit but needs to be drawn out, spiritually speaking, it's like drawing water from a well. This is similar to Gail's comment when she used the word "well" when she made the statement. I believe, because of our communication, that Gail accepts the information in this book, for me, but does not necessarily accept it for herself. Because of her position, I can only conclude that she was inspired to make the comment that encouraged me to write chapter 6. Several people, including Gail, have stated that chapter 6 was the most informative of all the chapters in this book. This observation indicates to me that a small miracle had occurred to inspire chapter 6. I also believe this inspiration has the character of God being expressed which consists of the mysterious, miraculous and unbelievable qualities. Proverbs 20:5 (TLB) **"Though good advise lies deep within a counselor's heart, the wise man will draw it out."**

When a person dies out to earthly beliefs, a whole new world dawns upon the individual. It's like a caterpillar confined to the earth until it emerges from its cocoon and begins a new life of flight, as a butterfly, no longer confined to the earth. Likewise, a spiritual person emerges form earthly issues, religious desires and controversial earthly causes. This new "birth" does not stop us from living; we simply change our attitude and beliefs. Basically, a spiritual person stops (indulging in earthly beliefs) pretending to know God and begins to (indulge in spiritual thoughts) seeking God's will and develops a desire to understand and follow his thoughts and reasoning instead of our own "earthly" thoughts and reasoning.

If we actually accept and believe that this natural world and this natural life that we human beings are engaged in, is just an illusion, then we must realize that we <u>are living a lie throughout this earthly existence.</u> If this is true, doesn't it make sense that our primary goal and attention should shift from the natural to the spiritual? This does not in any way imply that our life style should change, just our inner attitude. In the Bible, the book of John chapter 3, Jesus is explaining this attitude change to a religious leader named Nicodemus. John 3 verse 3 (TLB) ***"Jesus replied, with all the earnestness I possess I tell you this: Unless you are born again you can never get into the "Kingdom of God".*** And John3: 5-8 (TLB) ***<u>"what I am telling you so earnestly is this:</u> Unless one is born of water and the Spirit, he cannot enter the Kingdom of God, but the Holy Spirit gives new life from heaven; so don't be surprised at my statement that you must be born again!"*** This new birth is simply a change of attitude as indicated in the previous paragraph. Also entering into the Kingdom of God" is a present tense experience that is achieved by changing one's alliance from earthly concerns and earthly issues to heavily issues and heavenly concerns. We human beings are naturally born into this natural world and our natural nature is adapted to this lifestyle. This lifestyle is aimed towards trying to make our earthly life as bearable as possible. Part of achieving this goal is to be in denial. Yes, denial, we see the turmoil and strife going on around us but we focus on trying to cope with this chaotic world by attempting to change and control the terminal conditions of the world. Our natural instincts refuse to admit that we are fighting a loosing battle. Until we have a change of attitude, we are part of the problem and are unwilling and refuse to experience the new birth. We human beings have one primary goal and that is to focus on our earthly life. Everything we say and do is aimed at instant earthly gratification. Philippians 3:17-19 (TLB) ***"Dear brothers, pattern your lives after mine and notice who else lives up to my example. For I have told you often before, and I say it again now with tears in my eyes, there are many who walk along the Christian road who are really enemies of the cross of Christ. Their future is eternal loss, for their god (religion) is their appetite<u>: they are proud of what they should be ashamed of; and all they</u>***

think about is this life here on earth". (Patriotism or religion) When a person is born again, this new life simply focuses on a future life that has the opposite effect <u>"ashamed of what they used to be proud of."</u> The realization is that this world is a "temporary inconvenience". Those who do not agree with this philosophy and are still focused on the natural state of mind will naturally accuse the spiritual person of being a "cop-out" of life on earth and will hate the spiritual person because they don't agree or actively support these earthly beliefs and controversial issues. Romans 3:15 (TLB*)* ***"They are quick to kill hating anyone who disagrees with them."*** These earthly goals focus on the sanctity of governments, as in a patriotic support of governments and the sanctity of religions, as in pride of one's religion.

The Devil's character and goal is to keep humanity focused on our earthly life. The premise is that this natural existence is the only life we will ever know. The Devil wants everyone to believe that our religious and political ties are our only connection to eternity. Man purposes that "a wonderful proud memory is each individual's main purpose and accomplishment in this life and will be eternally important from generation to generation." But God has promised that even the memory of religious and political pride will be erased. Psalms 9:5-6(TLB) ***"You have rebuked the nations and destroyed the wicked, blotting out their names forever and ever. O enemies of mine you are doomed forever. The Lord will destroy your cities; <u>even the memory of them will disappear."</u>*** Also Psalms 9: 20 (TLB) ***"Make them tremble in fear; put the nations in their place until at last they know they are but puny men."*** Please try to understand; as long as we exist in this evil world and our natural evil nature desires this lifestyle, we are forced, outwardly, to support the government and its decisions. But spiritually speaking, every earthly government, without exception is contaminated with the evil nature. And human logic tells us, world governments, to some extent, are necessary to contain and hold in check the evil nature of man.

The primary fruits of the Spirit are Love, Joy, Peace, Faith and Hope. Probably the least of these fruits to be understood or accepted is Peace. Peace is the opposite of conflict. To be at peace with God simply means that there is no fear or apprehension, or doubt about our bond of love with God. The Oxford American Dictionary's interpretation of peace is: **'quiet, calm, peace of mind free from anxiety also a state of harmony between people, absence of strife."** Absence of strife and harmony between people, this is the ideal position a person wants between themselves and God. When a person achieves this condition of peace with God, then we are in a position to follow His instructions to enter into His rest. Hebrews 4:9-11 (TLB) *"So there is a full complete rest still waiting for the people of God, Christ has already entered there. He is resting from his work, just as God did after the creation. Let us do our best to go into that place of rest too, being careful not to disobey God---."* If we're not resting we are disobeying God. The Oxford American Dictionary interprets rest: **"to be still to cease from movement or action or working."** Here's another obvious conclusion, if you are religious or patriotic you are actively pursuing these ideals, likewise, if you not religious or patriotic you are inactive and could be at rest. Once again it should be obvious that rest is only possible if we have peace, likewise it should also be obvious that we cannot be actively involved with religious or patriotic activities and be at rest at the same time.

As I recall, an acquaintance, of my past, had requested that a particular song be sang at her funeral. The title of the song is: "Wonderful Peace" now imagine these words being sang at your funeral **"Far away in the depths of my Spirit tonight rolls a melody sweeter than psalms. In celestial like strains it unceasingly falls O're my soul like an infinite calm. Peace! Peace! Wonderful peace, coming down from the Father above; Sweep over my spirit forever, I pray in fathomless billows of love."** There are 4 more verses to this song emphasizing peace. This acquaintance believed that "wonderful peace" would finally be experienced after this terminal life had ended. Many people would consider this persons final request to be a glorious ending with a strong devotion of hope and faith. If we look at this testimony spiritually it will become clear that there was no peace prier to death. Galatians 5:22 (TLB) *"But when the Holy Spirit controls our lives <u>he will produce this kind of fruit in us:</u> love, joy, <u>peace</u>, patience, kindness, goodness, faithfulness, gentleness and self control--."* Without "peace" we cannot enter into God's place of rest. Can you see how this person has missed the previous instruction to "enter into God's place of rest? Hebrews 4:8-11 (TLB) *"This new place of rest he is talking about does not mean the land of Israel that Joshua led them into. If that were what God meant, he would not have spoken long afterwards about "today" being the time to get in. So there is a full complete rest still waiting for the people of God. Christ has already entered there. He is resting from his work, just as God did after the creation. <u>Let us do our best to go</u>*

into that place of rest, too, being careful not to disobey God as the children of Israel did, thus failing to get in" If our relationship with God is complete and totally compatible, while we are here on earth, we will have permanent peace now and forever. John 14:27 (TLB*) "I am leaving you with a gift—peace of mind and heart! And the peace I give isn't fragile like the peace the world gives. So don't be troubled or afraid."* Philippians 4:7 (TLB) *"If you do this you will experience God's peace, which is far more wonderful than the human mind can understand.* <u>*His peace will keep your thoughts and your hearts quite and at rest*</u> *as you trust in Christ Jesus."*

A few years ago I recall hearing a statement that went something like this **"understanding surpasses knowledge"**. If we analyze this statement it seems to make sense. If we only have knowledge of a subject it's like "carnal" information perhaps lacking substance or spiritual acknowledgment. If we accept, as fact and absorb the reasoning behind the knowledge into our psych the knowledge takes on character and becomes part of our being (understanding). The reason I brought up this subject is to emphasize the possibility that the information presented in this manuscript, could become an important part of our spiritual being. If we can accept as fact that this natural life we are experiencing is an illusion this will move us into the realm of "understanding" and we can then realize the reality of our situation. This does not stop us from living the illusion but in our spirit we know that our existence on earth is futile as far as God is concerned. At this point, in our understanding, it is then possible to admit spiritually that we are living a lie and that this natural life is, as the preacher said, futile. Ecclesiastes 12:8 (TLB) *"All is futile, says the Preacher; utterly futile.'* When we realize our situation then it becomes possible to be re-bon into the spiritual world. But the fallacy of the natural world must be realized (understood) before the re-birth can be experienced.

Some people may reason that this manuscript is no more truthful or important than any other theory being presented. In other words, what makes this book more real than the thousands of other philosophies of life? Probably the most compelling fact is that this writing focuses on God's spiritual world while all other theories that I know of, are based on this earthly life. The religions of the world try to bring God into this chaotic corrupt world, which implies that God is approving of our life style and also trying, but failing to make this deteriorating life a pleasant experience. It's totally disrespectful if we human beings imply that God is participating in this deathly existence. If we are able to accept the fact that our evil nature is in total and complete opposition to God then we will realize that our salvation (deliverance from earthly beliefs) is dependant on his constant power of grace (underserved favor). I do not believe in God, (in my natural being.) My very nature is to deny and doubt the existence of God. It is only the Spirit of God moving within my spirit that stirs my faith and allows me to be secure and assured of his acceptance of me. As the lyrics of a hymn goes **"Blessed assurance Jesus is mine Oh what a foretaste of glory divine—"** Yes it's the blessed assurance that allows me to believe in God's mercy. God must continually assure me of his saving grace. If the spirit of God does not continually assure me of his love I will stop believing. Psalms 33:22 (TLB) ***"Yes, Lord, let your constant love surround us, for our hopes are in you alone"***. If we could believe in God without his constant assurance, we wouldn't need his salvation. We would be fooling ourselves into thinking we could save ourselves. We would actually be pretending to know God. We may fool ourselves and other people in our lives but the important question is are we fooling God? Psalms 7:9 (TLB) ***"End all wickedness, O Lord, and bless all who truly worship God; for you, the righteous God, look deep within the hearts of men and examine all their motives and their thoughts"***.

I'm sure some people reading this book believe that my dislike for religion is my opinion based upon a bad experience, while participating in religion. I would only hope that any body with this thought would consider the possibility that their reasoning could be considered denial on their part. Religion is the breeding ground for producing pride. If a person is religious this person is also proud. Proverbs 16:5 (TLB) ***"Pride disgusts the Lord. Take my word for it—proud men shall be punished."*** Religion transforms a person into a wolf in sheep's clothing. They pretend to be caring, but in their heart, they are condemning anyone who does not agree with their beliefs. Religion exalts a person above all other human beings, just the opposite of being humble. Psalms 18:27 (TLB) ***"You deliver the humble but condemn the proud and haughty ones."*** Religion produces an aggressive image instead of a meek image. These aggressive characteristics are the opposite of what Jesus teaches us to be acceptable in the Kingdom of Heaven. If a person is religious this person cannot enjoy the peace and rest offered to those who respect and honor the teachings of Christ. If we are motivated by a religious or patriotic image we should try to realize that the intentions of these images are evil and as the saying goes **"the streets of Hell are paved with good intentions"** and these intentions denounce God's gift of salvation. The gift of salvation is spiritual deliverance from this evil corrupt world Matthew 6:24 (TLB) ***"You cannot serve two masters: God and money (religion). For you will hate one and love the other or else the other way around."*** Mark 8:35 (TLB) ***"if you insist on saving your life, (religion) you will lose it. <u>Only those who throw away their lives</u> (religion) for my sake and the sake of the Good News <u>will ever know what it means to really live.</u>"***

As stated in chapter 5, I am not trying to start a new religion and whether or not anybody accepts this information is out of my control. Of course I wish everybody could have the abundant assurance in the spirit that I have.

For the most part, life on earth, for me, has been a sad experience and I am continually mourning within my spirit. This mourning is the result of watching life deteriorate before my eyes as those I love suffer the pangs of a slow death. The up side is, I have the assurance that eternity will have the opposite effect.

God is not my helper, nor is He my co-pilot. He is my inspiration and pilot as he delivers (saves) me from this sinful world. My allegiance is not for any earthly government my allegiance is for eternal life. I look forward to a peaceful, joyful, loving eternity. Psalms 60:4-5 (TLB*)* ***"But you have given us a banner to rally to; all who love truth will rally to it; then you can deliver your beloved people. Use your strong right arm to rescue us."***

This natural world offers me conflict, war, chaos, hate, uncertainty, false hope and deception. The god of illusion controls this world. Now that I see the reality of the situation it is hard for me to believe that anybody could believe that a perfect God could be involved in such a hell. Anybody professing that God is participation in this natural disaster is also implying that God is "in- perfect." To believe that God is involved with this natural world is to dishonor God by making him a partner with the Devil. Because of the chaotic condition of this natural world, such an alliance would obviously make the Devil the head of this partnership. Of course God created this world and there is beauty in the creation but it has been contaminated by our fallen nature.

Another bazaar reality is why would a person confess their sins to a man? (Man of the cloth) The person you're confessing to needs salvation as much as you. We all, without exception, need salvation (deliverance from this evil world). Here's proof, Simon Peter, one of the main disciples, who was a constant companion of Jesus for the time Jesus was here on earth, denied even knowing Jesus, when Jesus was arrested, and crucified. If anybody throughout history had an opportunity to know Jesus it would be Simon Peter and yet after being with Jesus, throughout his ministry Jesus makes a statement on the night of his crucifixion. Luke 22:31-32 (TLB) ***"Simon, Simon, Satan has asked to have you, to sift you like wheat, but I have pleaded in prayer for you that your faith should not completely fail, So when you have repented and turned to me again, strengthen and build up the faith of your brothers."*** Part of this verse needs to be repeated, **"When you have repented and turned to me again, strengthen and build up the faith of your brothers."** What do you think? Is the next verse what Peter needs to repent of? Simon said, ***"Lord, I am ready to go to jail with you, and even to die with you."*** But Jesus said, ***Peter, let me tell you something between now and tomorrow morning when the rooster crows, you will deny me three times declaring that you don't even know me."*** Are we enlightened more than Peter? As you can see, by this example, we can clam to be faithful in our own strength but we would only be fooling ourselves. Many human beings believe that God will accept them into Heaven because of their devotion to religion. Matthew 7:22 (TLB) ***"At the Judgment many will tell me, Lord, Lord, we told others about you and used your name to cast out demons and to do many other great miracles." But I will reply, "You have never been mine. Go away, for your deeds are evil."*** (Religious pride)

Hears one of my final truths. "I'm afraid of dying I have doubts about "life after death" I do everything I can to put off dying, I exercise, take vitamins watch my diet and I dread the thought of death. However, at the same time, in my spirit, I 'm actually "homesick" for heaven. To me this final comment has <u>the mysterious, miraculous and unbelievable character of God</u>. It's <u>unbelievable</u> to think a person could be afraid of dying and at the same time be "homesick for heaven." It's <u>mysterious</u> that such a plan could contain these opposite feelings together. These events can only be described as a miracle. Psalms 136:23 (TLB) ***"He remembered our utter weakness, for his loving kindness continues forever."***

"Like salmon fulfilling their destiny by migrating upstream against the currents of water to eventually spawn, we must struggle against a world of unbelief to find fulfillment and eventually discover eternal life."

The most noteworthy and popular Salmon, in fresh water lakes, of the northern United States Reagan are where this popular Salmon reach their birthplace, spawn and die before their eggs hatch. When the eggs hatch an inborn instinctive force, throughout their lives, guides the hatchlings. The hatchlings start their lives as fresh water fish. After a few months the Salmon start a treacherous journey down stream and eventually end up in the Ocean as salt-water fish. After a few years the Salmon leave the salt-water environment and revert back to fresh water fish and start the treacherous journey back upstream to their original birthplace. Scientists have also discovered that Salmon will strike at bate but mysteriously stop eating when they start their unbelievable, miraculous migration and their appearance takes a drastic metamorphism.

Even though the life cycle of the Salmon takes approximately six years this miraculous migration takes place every year. How is it passable for Salmon to migrate each year when their life cycle is approximately every six years? This question should stretch the imagination, to the breaking point, of evolutionists.

What is the purpose of these mysterious, unbelievable and miraculous changes that the Salmon go through? We humans have the ability to reason and ponder this phenomenon; therefore the life cycle of Salmon is obviously for our benefit, to get a glimpse into God's ability to go against the laws of nature in His creative abilities and as proof of His miraculous, mysterious and unbelievable personality. If there is a better explanation I would like to know about it.

When a person becomes spiritual they will begin to focus on a "spiritual migration," like the Salmon when they stop eating, a spiritual person may voice an opinion,(strike) but will not actively support (consume) earthly ideologies and their outlook on life takes on a drastic metamorphism, of this earthly life, as they concentrate on the inner force leading to eternal life.

I see light (LIFE) at the end of the tunnel. "Row, row, row your boat, gently down the stream, merrily, merrily, merrily, merrily, life is but a dream."

P.S. Anybody with the ability to translate this book into other languages has the author's permission to do so. This book is also available on an audible copy. For comments and questions contact the author Charlie Walton at-----Non Fiction   P.O. Box 40378   Grand Junction Colo. 81504

Made in the USA
Columbia, SC
10 July 2024